The First Sino-Japanese War: The History and Legacy of the Conflict that Doomed the Chinese Empire and Led to the Rise of Imperial Japan
By Charles River Editors

A British cartoon depicting the smaller Japan defeating the bigger China

About Charles River Editors

Charles River Editors is a boutique digital publishing company, specializing in bringing history back to life with educational and engaging books on a wide range of topics. Keep up to date with our new and free offerings with this 5 second sign up on our weekly mailing list, and visit Our Kindle Author Page to see other recently published Kindle titles.

We make these books for you and always want to know our readers' opinions, so we encourage you to leave reviews and look forward to publishing new and exciting titles each week.

Introduction

A picture of Japanese soldiers during the war

The First Sino-Japanese War

Completing the Meiji Restoration that heralded the dawn of a new era for both Japan and Asia, the island nation found itself thrust into the modern world, a world of industry and conquest. Flexing its new muscles, the burgeoning power soon came to blows with the regional power that for centuries dominated the area politically and culturally: China. Also seeking to modernize in the wake of Western exploitation, China struggled to adapt to the changing times, doing everything it could to maintain a balance between modernity and tradition. Japan found that balance, and, its new industry desperate for raw materials, looked to the peninsula of Korea for new markets and resources. China, in contrast, refused to strike such a balance, adopting a veneer of modernity while maintaining the status quo, both domestically and with regards to Korea.

For decades Korea existed as a protectorate of China, paying homage to the mighty Chinese dynasties while minding its own business as best it could. However, sensing weakness in the former regional power after being defeated by the Europeans during the Second Opium War, escalating tensions over Korea between the old power of China and the new power of Japan led to the First Sino-Japanese War. In its first modern war, the modernized Japanese empire went to war against the dominant power in the region, and though interested Western powers favored China, Japan won the day, claiming Korea as their conquest and permanently upsetting the balance of power in the region. The conflict paved the way for the future Empire of Japan and the collapse of the Qing Dynasty.

Though both nations modernized, and China far outweighed Japan in terms of men and materiel potential, the island nation handily won its first modern war. Why did the smaller Japan defeat the formerly mighty Qing Dynasty? What did both nations glean from the war? What did Western powers, watching the ancient dragon battle the upstart tiger, think of the war? The answers to these questions reflect both Japan's short-term gains in the wake of victory, and the long term disaster for both sides' new roles in Asia. For with the end of Chinese dominance in East Asia came a new era for the region as a whole, an era whose consequences and horrors would not be fully realized for several more decades.

The First Sino-Japanese War: The History and Legacy of the Conflict that Doomed the Chinese Empire and Led to the Rise of Imperial Japan looks at how the two sides went to war, as well as the crucial aftermath. Along with pictures and a bibliography, you will learn about the First Sino-Japanese War like never before.

The First Sino-Japanese War: The History and Legacy of the Conflict that Doomed the Chinese Empire and Led to the Rise of Imperial Japan

About Charles River Editors

Introduction

   Between the Dragon and the Tiger

   Expanding the Military

   The Declaration of War

   The First Sino-Japanese War

   Foreign Perspectives

   Peace Negotiations

   The Aftermath of War

   Online Resources

   Further Reading

Free Books by Charles River Editors

Discounted Books by Charles River Editors

Between the Dragon and the Tiger
Following Japan's entry into the modern world in the late 19th century, the newly industrialized nation struggled to change the way it dealt with its neighbors. China, formerly the dominant power in the region, already looked like a pale imitation of its once mighty dynasties, due to Western exploitation. In 1871 Japan attempted to negotiate a Western themed treaty with China, only to be rebuffed by the weak, but not defeated, nation.[i]

For centuries, China loomed as the cultural and economic center of East Asia. In fact, Japanese culture and language derived heavy influence from the continent, Korea paid homage to the Chinese dynasties, and even Thailand acknowledged Chinese might of arms and art. The Qing Dynasty would not relinquish such prestige easily, especially to what it considered a backwater island nation of barbarians.

Rebuffed by the still influential, if not as powerful, China, Japan looked to smaller targets to assert its new role in the region – unique amongst the Asian countries, Japan managed to peacefully treat with Western powers and modernize, with only a relatively minor civil war impeding their advance toward modernity.[ii] Thanks to distractions closer to home, coupled with the more organized and centralized power of Japan's tiny island Empire, it maintained cordial, if uneven, relations with Western powers.

Also focusing closer to home, in 1874 Japan flexed its muscles by launching a punitive raid on Taiwan, a costly venture that proved more trouble than it was worth.[iii] For Japan, such an act reeked of the growing pains of an empire caught between massive China, which was still recovering from a recent lengthy rebellion, and Western powers, which accepted Japanese independence but still looked down on them because of their Asian ethnicity.[iv]

Acknowledging that China was still too big to fight, Japan shifted its focus to a smaller, easier target: Korea. Like China, Korea was known to the Japanese and had maintained limited relations while the island nation isolated itself from the bulk of the outside world during the Tokugawa Shogunate. Like Japan, Korea received a great deal of cultural influence from Japan, and it had been a protectorate of China's for centuries, paying homage to their dynasties while Korean rulers did their best to get on with things. But even as Korea kept the outside world at bay for the most part, the Chinese colossus and Japanese upstart proved too stubborn and powerful for the small peninsular nation to rebuff.[v] In 1876, Japan pushed Korea into accepting an unequal trade agreement, similar to ones forced upon China by Western powers. Japan also annexed the Ryukyu Islands to the south in 1879, despite the islands being claimed by China as a protectorate.[vi] Japan focused more on Korea than to surrounding islands because of its proximity, and because of the history of relations between the two nations, a history that stretched back to the beginnings of the Shogunate.[vii] At that time Korea stood, theoretically at least, on equal esteem as the Shogun, the military ruler of Japan during the time.[viii] With the Emperor reasserting his authority in the wake of the Meiji Restoration, it stood to reason that Korea now held a subservient status to Japan, as far as Japanese diplomatic thinking went.[ix]

Despite the Meiji Restoration, the growing pains of the modernizing nation became apparent during a series of Korean civil disturbances in 1882 and 1884. Having sent advisors to Korea as part of the 1876 treaty, Japan watched Korea experience its own pains of modernization.[x] The rapid thrusting of Korea into international trade without the proper adaptations in industry and government led to urban inflation and rising resentment, both toward the royal court and foreign legations.[xi] In 1882, rioters attacked the Japanese delegation and the Korean Royal Court. It took an intervention by the Chinese Army to suppress the rioters and restore order, aptly demonstrating that despite Japan's grandstanding, China remained an influential force in Korea and Asia at large.[xii]

To maintain order in their protectorate, the Chinese government stationed troops in Seoul, Korea's capital. Already divided between supporters of China and Japan, in 1884, pro-Japanese Koreans attempted a coup against their Chinese protectors. The Japanese delegation sided with the rebels, but Japan's government remained neutral, and the Chinese military quickly crushed the revolt.[xiii] Despite vocal desires in Japan to take Korea, the government worked diplomatically with China, and their neutrality during the uprising managed to prevent an international incident.[xiv]

In 1885, the same year China concluded a brief war with France, its government and Japan's reached an agreement regarding Korea. Known as the Tientsin, or Tianjin, Convention, this agreement stated that both nations would pull their military forces from Korea within four months. It also encouraged the Korean government to hire third-party advisors to modernize its military, and, most important for the future of all three nations, the agreement stated, "In case [of] any disturbances of a grave nature occurring in Corea (sic) which necessitates the respective countries, or either of them, to send troops to Corea (sic), it is hereby understood that they shall give, each to the other, previous notice in writing of their intention so to do, and that after the matter is settled they shall withdraw their troops and not further station them there."[xv]

With little regard for Korea itself, the burgeoning Empire of Japan and the aging Qing Dynasty decided the fate of the peninsular nation. No longer solely under Chinese protection, the small kingdom found itself trapped between two regional powers.

Still, with the rioters and revolutionaries suppressed, order restored, and Korea in theory on the path to modernization like the rest of Asia, peace seemed secure in the region for the moment. Having clearly seen the failings of their burgeoning (not to mention small) military, the Japanese government went to work continuing to adapt and modernize. China, struggling to keep Western powers at bay, attempted to do the same.[xvi] How each nation continued to modernize would foreshadow the following war, and thus the very fate of East Asia overall.

Expanding the Military

Japan's military failures in Korea and Taiwan, as well as China's defeat against France and other European powers, demonstrated to both the need to modernize and expand their militaries, including equipment, organization, and logistical coordination. Japan in particular looked to the lessons the West taught the Chinese, while the Chinese struggled to modernize while maintaining their dominant cultural identity in the region, a position slowly eroded by the French and British.

However, even as both Japan and China took a hard look at their roles in Asia following their entry into the greater world, they took very different courses of action. Japan, with a warrior class and firm footing as a modern, industrialized nation, looked to oppose Western encroachment and secure a more dominant role in Asia.[xvii] For Japan, a secure future relied upon building up and keeping its military modernized.

In 1873, Japan passed a universal male conscription act, a move that undermined the samurai class from their lofty position in Japanese society as warrior elite, though their respected position of nobility remained ingrained in the culture even as the feudal structure of Japan was dismantled with the earlier Restoration.[xviii] This first conscription in Japan was not only unpopular with the still prominent samurai families, rural people also resisted, and many young men utilized a variety of methods to avoid military service, with some going as far as hiding out north in secluded Hokkaido.[xix] Ironically, the conscription law, advocated by future general Yamagata Aritomo, was based on a French model at the time and held several exemptions for service. Worded as it was, the bulk of military duty fell on the second and younger sons of agrarian families, with firstborn sons being one of the main exemptions of the law.[xx]

Aritomo

In 1883, the conscription system was revised to reduce exemptions and incorporate a three level structure, sorted into three years of active service, four years in the first reserve, and five years in the second reserve.[xxi] The ease for the wealthy to reduce their service time remained, however, and discontent festered due to the unequal nature of the army.[xxii] What followed, despite later reform efforts in 1889, was an army of poor farmers' children led by the leftover elites of a society who looked down on their own soldiers with disdain.

China also attempted to adapt their military to the 19th century. However, the Chinese were so steeped in tradition that they refused to advance and reform on a united front in any sense, whether militarily, domestically, or politically. A handful of reformers in the 19th century, roughly at the same time as the Meiji Restoration, struggled to reform China, including its military.[xxiii] Though they achieved limited success, the military's development lagged behind even Japan's, as the Chinese government emphasized Western technology to eschew proper military reforms –reforms that would necessitate political reforms, something the government sought to avoid.[xxiv] Thus, while Japan modernized politically and culturally, China merely adopted a modern façade, one whose coating revealed to be very thin indeed.

The creation of the Japanese Diet in 1890 further complicated matters. With a Westernized government to match its new military, Japan found its martial spirit eroding due to conscription issues, a government interested only in political games, and a people not nearly as united as their long history should indicate.[xxv] To truly gauge its modernity, the nation would have to thrust itself into the greatest unifier of peoples and nations: war.

With conscription in effect, the Japanese government needed a modernized military framework to muster, document, train, and station those troops, and to keep tabs on the reservists should they need to answer a call to arms.[xxvi] For such an effort, both Japan and China relied on foreign advisors to aid the transition from a feudal society to a modern one in the case of Japan, and as mentioned earlier, to avoid the need for internal reforms in the case of China.

During the Meiji Restoration, French advisors were some of the most prominent, and that prominence remained as Japan continued to modernize.[xxvii] However, the French defeat in 1871 by the newly formed German Empire brought a new set of advisors and military model to prominence. German-educated Katsura Taro advocated a German-based military system in the wake of Japan's military failings under the French model, and with the help of German advisors, Japan's army rebuilt itself from a domestically military model similar to a police force into a modern divisional army prepared to fight on foreign soil.[xxviii] The changes to the conscription to reflect reservist tiers, noted previously, stand out as one such influence of the German advisors.

Taro

While the army reformed and reorganized, the navy also modernized. Unfortunately, with Japanese industry not quite up to par, Japan, like China, was heavily dependent on the purchase of foreign-built ships, or at the very least ships paid for and built in foreign yards.[xxix] As both branches of the military reformed, they started working together during war drills to form a cohesive military force.[xxx] How effective such a force would be until tested in the crucible of war remained to be seen.

At the same time, political and military turmoil combined to create an unstable situation many believed could only be resolved through the unifying power of war. Japan's representative in London received word in March of 1894, "If we don't have something to distract the people's attention, we won't be able to quieten this ferment…."[xxxi] For the first time in Japan's history, public and international opinion mattered; a modern nation, especially an upstart one considered racially inferior by the world powers in Europe, could not start a war without a pretext, thin as it might be.

Forces outside Japan also pressured the nation to take the step towards its modern war. Russia, a massive empire sprawling across two continents, started construction, in 1891, of the Trans-Siberian Railway. The 6,000-miles railway would run from Moscow to Vladivostok, Russia's only warm water port on the Pacific Ocean.[xxxii] The two nations had come to blows in the past, even in the time of the Shogunate, and a railway to expand Pacific trade also meant, as far as the Japanese were concerned, an expansion of Russian power into Asia. The Russians might also threaten to stretch their influence into China and the Pacific Ocean.[xxxiii]

The Japanese government feared Russian encroachment in China, but few believed the haphazardly modernizing dynasty could fend off the Russian Bear for long. Thus, most figured the best way to repel the Tsar's expansion was a foothold on the Asian mainland to counter Russian advances.[xxxiv] However, any hostile move on the mainland would surely incite war with China, and, possibly with Russia as well. Though unlikely, the prospect of a Russian-Chinese alliance against Japan raised enough concern to warrant probes for a Sino-Japanese alliance against Russia.[xxxv]

Those probes ended in 1893 following two reports from Japanese military personnel touring China at the time. Both personnel concluded that China's military and industrial development was not nearly as complete or encompassing as Japan's, and they further reported rampant opium abuse.[xxxvi] Naturally, while these reports ended talks of a Sino-Japanese alliance, they did ease Japan's concerns about the difficulties of establishing a foothold on the mainland, even as Yamagata tried to remind leaders, "Neither China nor Korea is our enemy: it is Britain, France, Russia."[xxxvii]

Regardless, the stage was set for Japan's first modern war, as its growing ambitions in Asia coincided with China's weakening. All the island empire needed to expand further was a pretext for war, and once again, the casus belli for that Asian war would be the small, peninsula kingdom stuck between two other powerful nations jostling for dominance.

The Declaration of War

Japan, now beholden to public and international opinion, with several European powers in the region to the south and north, needed a proper pretense to go to war on the mainland. Korea provided that pretense, and Japan and China's reactions would set the stage for Asian politics for decades.

In January of 1894, Korean peasants exploited by their lords joined with a rising religious movement to start a civil war. The Donghak Peasant Revolution quickly gathered followers discontent with their exploitation by the nobility and foreign merchants.[xxxviii] Unable to quell the growing revolt, the Korean king requested military intervention from China in early June, and in accordance with the treaty of 1885, the Chinese government informed Japan that "it is in harmony with our constant practice to protect our tributary states by sending our troops to assist them…"[xxxix]

The dispatch's dismissive attitude towards Korea as a nation, coupled with Japan's belief in its own dominance over the peninsular kingdom, gave the Japanese government enough pretense to intervene. With a mixture of imperial benevolence not unlike the White Man's Burden of late 19th century Britain, Japan mobilized the 5th Division (Hiroshima) on June 5, one day after the Korean request for aid.[xl] A week later, in a mobilization effort that would have no doubt impressed their German advisors, Japanese soldiers landed at Inchon, the closest port to Seoul. It was a port that would see itself used as a foothold more than once in the future.[xli]

Ironically, the war that aimed to gain prestige and the goodwill of the Western powers only incensed the latter. Great Britain, about to sign a revised treaty with Japan, had many vested interests in China. The British balked, and the American government insisted Japan would be held responsible for what happened to Korea in an unjust war.[xlii] Forces at home worked to propel the war forward, however, because Japanese history suggested that backing down could lead to public pressure and even possibly incite a revolt by the old samurai families.[xliii]

Despite the seeming need for a war in the eyes of the government and military, the people's initial view of the war was ambivalent.[xliv] Some in the Japanese military looked warily to China as tensions mounted prior to open warfare, but a British observer seemed more optimistic about Japanese prospects, writing, "I came to Japan expecting to see some miserable parody of a third-rate European soldier; instead I find an army in every sense of the word admirably organized, splendidly equipped, thoroughly drilled, and strangest thing of all in Oriental people, cheaply and honestly administered… the Japanese army bears comparison with the Chinese much in the same way as the forces of 19th century civilization compare with those of medieval times."[xlv]

British snark notwithstanding, the Japanese army's veneer of modernity was almost as much a problem as China's. The soldiers were undernourished, stood at an average height of just over 5 feet (which was short even at that time in Asia), were equipped with single shot rifles in an era of multi-firing bolt actions, and lacked any modern battleships in its navy. Needless to say, the Japanese military faced a daunting task,[xlvi] and an editorial from a Japanese newspaper summed up the potential consequences of the war quite nicely: "If by some chance we blunder, what then? The worry is unbearable… this is an overseas war, something unknown to our ancestors these three centuries and quite different to earlier internal disturbances. Whatever happens, whatever the difficulties, our nation's forty millions are resolved not to withdraw one step until exhausted, and, whatever the cost, to prevail."[xlvii]

In early July of 1894, Japan wired China to form a joint reform movement for Korea, knowing China would refuse. When China did, Japan declared war on August 1. The Korean revolt used as an excuse by the Japanese military had been mostly suppressed by then, but as far as the Japanese military and government were concerned, the die was cast.[xlviii] Japan entered this war divided by old class hierarchies, political squabbles, and an untested military, so it's no surprise that China, the ancient center of culture and power in the region, despite being battered as it was by the West, was confident of success.

The First Sino-Japanese War

At first glance, the two nations had nearly as much going for them as against them. Both nation's militaries had outdated equipment even by the standards of the time, China's military organization was an insult to the word, and Japan's military, while much better organized, lacked full coordination, with troops moving to and fro without commanding officers knowing who was going where, or when.[xlix]

China's chief advantage was, of course, its size, as the Chinese population was three times its adversary's size. Moreover, the Japanese were concerned that Western powers, most notably Great Britain, Russia, and the United States, might intervene in the war at some point. The British had substantial financial interests in China, Russia's railroad threatened both sides, and America wanted to keep China open and to ingratiate itself with Korea, an endeavor in which it was largely successful during this time.[l] Any one of those powers interceding on behalf of China or Korea would nip Japan's war effort in the bud, and likely complicate matters for decades to come.

In the crucial first months of the war, Japan quickly mapped out its grand strategy, consolidating its foothold and organizing the chain of command. For the moment, the military ran the show, while the diplomats waited their turn as the army and navy prepared for their first true tests of arms.[li] While preparing this strategy, Yamagata, denied a field command due to his age, published a warning to the armed forces to avoid disunity. He declared the need for close cooperation between the military and civilian authorities, ensuring a unity in orders between both groups. He also advised everyone at the front, from military officers to diplomats, not to overstep their commands.[lii]

It did not take long for the war's goals to shift. Nominally declared to secure Korean independence, or at least Korean subservience to Japan instead of China, the war's objectives quickly escalated to include a strike into China's heartland.[liii] What the Japanese military planned was nothing less than the removal of China's position in the region as the primary power, and Japan's ascendance to that position. To do this, the military planned a joint naval-army strategy that would see the navy secure the Yellow Sea and Gulf of Chihli, allowing Japanese troops and materiel to travel freely from Japan into Korea.[liv] Once that water route was secured, the army would hold the Chinese in Korea and then strike directly at China, an offensive plan making modified use of the German strategy of striking quickly against a larger foe before they could fully mobilize their forces to counterattack or even form a proper defense.[lv] As a backup plan, should the untested but nominally superior Chinese Beiyang Fleet force beat back the equally untested and theoretically inferior Japanese navy, the troops in Korea would hold off the Chinese to secure a Korea independent from China.[lvi] The potential occupation of Taiwan also entered the picture, a seeming aside that would have more lasting consequences than originally anticipated.[lvii]

While politicians, diplomats, and generals coordinated, the Japanese civilian population anxiously anticipated news from the front, news made possible thanks to the newest media to spread through Japan: the newspaper. Japan's first foreign war also contained its first war correspondents,[lviii] as 129 reporters from 66 newspapers across the island nation entered the war zone to report to the home front, among them the renowned novelist Okamoto Kido.[lix] Kido's reports, like any good correspondent's, started on the boat to Inchon, where he reported on the amusing but pointed clothing mixture his fellow correspondents donned to enter the war zone: "The correspondents boarded the convoy ships at Ujina and were transported to Pusan or Inchon. This was a first experience for everyone and as there were no rules and regulations concerning the correspondents accompanying the troops, each had his own ideas about how to dress for the occasion. They wore Western clothing, but some among them wrapped white cotton sashes around their bellies into which they thrust long Japanese swords…. Reflecting upon it now, it seems comic, but back then correspondents had no way of knowing how much protection they might receive from the troops once they arrived at the front….. Even though they were supposed to be non-combatants, they had to keep their guard up…. In fact, at the time they had to be vigilant not just towards the Chinese troops, but towards the Korean people as well, so they had to put up a fairly fierce-looking front. Nor did the army personnel do anything in particular to discourage them."[lx] With the modern press being a rather new addition to Japanese society, the reporters sent to Korea included an eclectic bunch of writers and other literary fellows, as the field of journalism was too young to possess full-fledged reporters.[lxi]

Besides this mix of present and future literary men, the soldiers themselves also wrote of their time at the front, recording their thoughts when not in the midst of battle.[lxii] One such set of notes was published after the war. Titled *Episodes of the Korean Campaign* when translated, the bestseller illuminated the Korean people to Japanese eyes for the first time, making clear that as much as they desired the subservience of their neighbor, they still knew relatively little about their prospective protectorate.[lxiii] From such writings came an unflattering report of a people veneered in civilization but living in poverty and filth, with the author writing that there was "no hovel in the most barbaric interior of Africa as defiled; neither would the most barbarous tribesmen of Mongolia find such dwellings to live in."[lxiv]

Despite the declaration of war not occurring until August 1, the first major battles of the war took place beforehand. At Seonghwan two days earlier, 40,000 Japanese troops, aiming to secure the Korean capital of Seoul, faced off against a similar number of Chinese soldiers.[lxv] The Chinese, entrenched to defend against the Japanese assault, faced a flanking maneuver from the Japanese and, after less than three hours of intense fighting, fled the battlefield, surrendering Seoul to Japan for the remainder of the war.[lxvi]

The naval war started even earlier, on July 25, when the Japanese engaged a portion of the Beiyang Fleet loaded with reinforcements. The enemy flotilla included a British transport full of Chinese soldiers, and when it was sunk by the Japanese, only the British crew was rescued from the wreckage.[lxvii] Though the media situation at the time diffused tensions between East and West, Japan thus started the war under increased Western scrutiny.[lxviii]

A French depiction of British sailors being rescued

For the first three weeks of the war, Japanese troops slowly coalesced around Seoul. Bad roads and poor logistical support, combined with disease, took their toll on the army, but the Chinese, demoralized by the loss at Seonghwan and still recovering, failed to take advantage of the enemy's thin lines and weakened state.[lxix]

Once finally amassed, Japan's army prepared to strike at the next major Chinese base, Pyongyang.[lxx] The hasty move northward was due both to Japan's strategy for a rapid advance and the need to strike before the Chinese forces properly organized their superior numbers.[lxxi]

The Battle of Pyongyang, fought on September 15th, was a brief but harsh battle. Again, it was covered by war correspondents, and one of their reports give a detailed account of the battle: "As I arrived, our artillery had set up a gun emplacement about six or seven hundred metres to my rear and battle commenced between their guns and ours. Our shells came skimming only ten metres above my head, while those of the enemy passed no more than twenty to thirty metres above and occasionally landed around me. I took temporary refuge in a Korean graveyard but a couple of enemy shells landed there, hurling sand and earth into my face. There was no going forward or back. Whether they could see our artillerymen or not, the enemy turned all their guns on our emplacement, and the shells flew over like pouring rain…At the point, our Wonsan detachment had pushed as far as the right flank of our Sakunei detachment and the shouts of war were all around me. The Sakunei detachment finally seized the forward high ground and I used this as my opportunity to get away from the cemetery, going up to just behind the advance units. The men under Colonel Sato had already turned on the enemy's left wing fort, those under Major Yamaguchi the right wing fort. Our guns were placed as before and concentrated their fire on the central fortress."[lxxii]

As in the previous battle at Seonghwan, the two forces were not as uneven as either nation's size would suggest - Japan's forces numbered roughly around 12,000 soldiers, while the Chinese had anywhere from 15,000-20,000, depending on the source.[lxxiii] The Japanese outgunned the Chinese with 44 artillery guns to 28, and the casualties reflect that, as the Japanese officially suffered 108 dead, 506 wounded, and 12 missing, while the Chinese suffered over 2,000 dead and 600 captured.[lxxiv]

The statistics hide the true difficulties the Japanese overcame, as they were exhausted, underfed, dehydrated, and nearly out of ammo when they assaulted and forced back their entrenched enemy. Time and again the Chinese repulsed the Japanese advances, and it was only by flanking the Chinese rear that the Japanese army prevailed.[lxxv]

A depiction of the Japanese routing the Chinese at the battle

Shortly after that victory, the Japanese navy triumphed against the infamous Beiyang Fleet in the Yellow Sea. The fighting, which started on September 17, would be the first major test for each side, with the Chinese sporting state-of-the art German built warships and the Japanese fielding primarily British vessels, either built or bought to supplement their own.[lxxvi] Despite theoretical technological superiority, the Chinese navy suffered from archaic command structure and coordination, and much like the rest of the Qing Dynasty, a thin veneer of modernity masked the outdated institutions of the past.[lxxvii] Conversely, the Japanese had adapted its command structure along with its naval forces, allowing better coordination among their smaller vessels.

In the ensuing battle, the Chinese flagship, the German built *Dingyuan,* suffered over 700 shell hits, yet remained afloat. Other vessels did not fare as well, but the fleet remained a viable fighting force, and their flagship could be repaired to re-enter the fray. The Chinese commander, however, using archaic defensive tactics, retreated to defend the headquarters at Weihaiwei.[lxxviii] With the pride of the Chinese navy now hiding in the safety of their headquarters, the seas effectively belonged to Japan, ensuring troops and supplies could reach Korea unimpeded, and from there, the march to China continued.

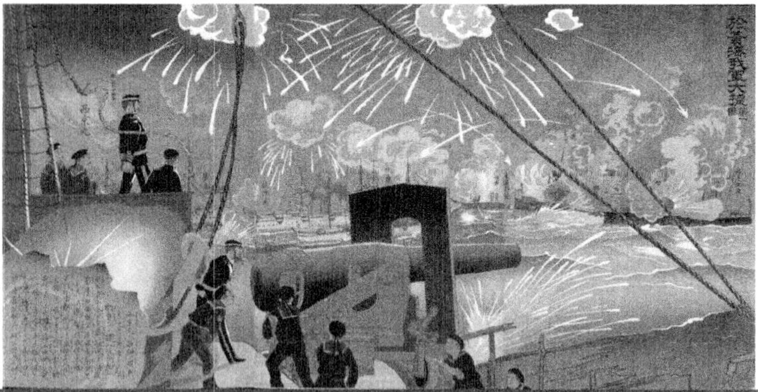
於黄海我軍大捷

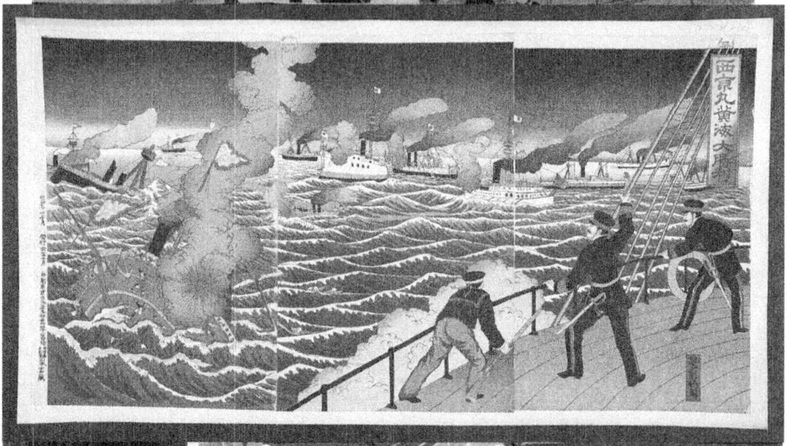

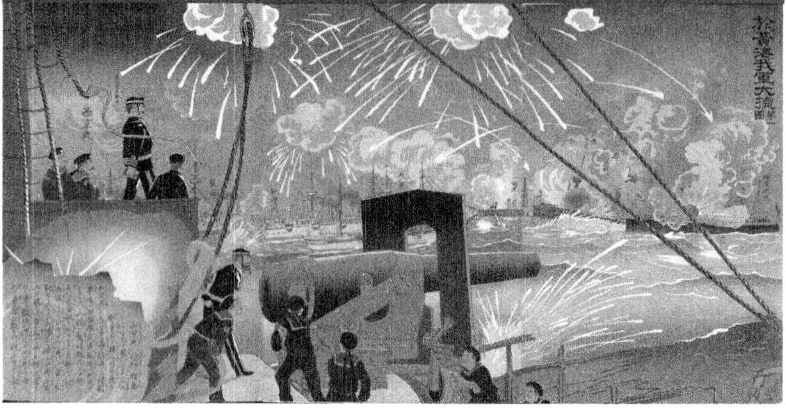
於黄海我軍大捷

Japanese depictions of the naval fighting

Despite Japanese logistical problems, Chinese forces continued pulling northward all the way to the border with Manchuria. By October 23, the Japanese Army reached the Yalu River, the natural border between Manchuria and Korea.[lxxix] Chinese troops amassed in Manchuria, but their intent to defend against a Japanese invasion seemed clear as they waited on the other side of the river. By that night, Japanese troops prepared to push the Chinese further back, crossing in the cover of darkness to encircle the enemy while erecting bridges to cross the river directly.[lxxx] By daybreak, the Japanese secured a foothold with high ground, and the Chinese, lacking adequate defense works, pulled back to regroup. The Battle of Jiuliancheng, also referred to as the Battle of the Yalu River, had begun.[lxxxi]

On the 26th, the Japanese, enduring heavy Chinese fire, managed to once again flank the Chinese troops and force them back, pushing them further into Manchuria. The Japanese followed, and once more the Chinese pulled back, this time without firing a single shot of resistance, though they did burn the nearby village down to deny it to the logistically strained enemy.[lxxxii] With the bitter cold of the region fully felt, and winter looming ever closer, the Japanese halted on November 1 at the torched village to regroup and bivouac for the winter.

While the army consolidated its position and worked out its logistical kinks, the diplomats worked to establish relations with the locals, as Japan now found itself an occupation force in its corner of Manchuria.[lxxxiii] Military and civilian officials butted heads frequently, sometimes even violently, forcing their superiors to promote and relocate officials - civilian and military alike - in order to diffuse tensions and present a united front against their Chinese foes.[lxxxiv] Meanwhile, the encamped forces prepared to march toward Beijing, a daunting prospect given that Japan's logistical issues remained a problem, and there would be a massive Chinese army waiting to greet them. Despite a constant string of defeats, the Qing's forces remained mostly intact thanks to their refusal to fight pitched battles.[lxxxv] If ever there was a location for a final stand, the Chinese capital would be the place.

As Japanese forces remained in Manchuria, the theater of war shifted to Port Arthur. Port Arthur guarded the water route to Beijing, meaning that if it fell, resupplying any advance or besieging force would become much easier, thereby easing the strain on the stretched Japanese logistics and securing another morale boosting victory for the Japanese.[lxxxvi]

In early November, Japanese forces pushed forward to take the port. The harbor protected by the fort fell November 21st, but street fighting continued for several days in the city itself,[lxxxvii] and as often happens in urban warfare, the lines between soldier and civilian were blurred. According to the Japanese, Qing soldiers removed their uniforms and continued fighting after the harbor fell. Conversely, the Chinese insisted the Japanese shot civilians, and the street fighting in Port Arthur, during which indiscriminate artillery caused civilian casualties, came to be known as the Port Arthur Massacre.[lxxxviii]

Controversies aside, the capture of Port Arthur was seen by many as the greatest victory up to that point for the Japanese. The port loomed in the minds of several prominent diplomats and generals as a defensive fortress comparable to Gibraltar or Constantinople before the invention of cannons, so the fact it fell so easily demonstrated the capabilities of the Japanese military, or at least so the thinking went.[lxxxix]

Back home, news of the brutality of urban warfare tainted the victory. Correspondents reported the grisly nature of such combat, with one report informing readers, "Their corpses piled into mountains, their blood flowing as rivers, many enemy soldiers came to a pathetic end after attempts to continue their resistance by disguising themselves as civilians. Bodies of the enemy lay everywhere in the roads and streets of the city. There are very few surviving Chinese in the area, and while they too are undoubtedly enemy combatants, as long as they offer no further resistance our forces are merciful and leave them alone."[xc]

Writing for the *New York World*, James Creelman told Americans, "The Japanese troops entered Port Arthur on Nov. 21 and massacred practically the entire population in cold blood. ... The defenseless and unarmed inhabitants were butchered in their houses and their bodies were unspeakably mutilated. There was an unrestrained reign of murder which continued for three days. The whole town was plundered with appalling atrocities. ... It was the first stain upon Japanese civilization. The Japanese in this instance relapsed into barbarism."

For their part, Japanese correspondents repeatedly toned down or ignored civilian causalities, doing their best to blunt the horrors of urban warfare and play up the idea of Chinese partisans over the simple indiscriminate nature of artillery in a confined space.[xci] Japan's Foreign Ministry asserted, "The Japanese Government desires no concealment of the events at Port Arthur. On the contrary, it is investigating rigidly for the purpose of fixing the exact responsibility and is taking measures essential to the reputation of the empire. ... Japanese troops transported with rage at the mutilation of their comrades by the enemy, broke through all restraints ... [and] exasperated by the wholesale attempts [by Chinese soldiers] at escape disguised at citizens, they inflicted vengeance without discrimination. ... the victims, almost without exception, were soldiers wearing the stolen clothes of citizens."

As a result, the Port Arthur Massacre faded into a historical footnote, and the lessons of its atrocities were never learned, which would lead to similar incidents among the Japanese and Chinese in the 1930s.

As 1894 ended, the war was clearly going in favor of Japan, with Port Arthur occupied, Japanese forces deep in Manchuria, and the Chinese navy hiding in port.[xcii] However, plenty of observers figured this position could easily turn, given that Chinese forces remained relatively intact. The port could fall to the Chinese navy, and the Japanese forces in Manchuria could still be surrounded and wiped out. Given that they vastly outnumbered the Japanese, plenty of people still thought the Chinese would turn the tables in 1895, push back the Japanese, and win the day.

In fact, the initial stages of 1895 quickly upset Japan's grand strategy. The plan to thrust at the Chinese capital to quickly end the war had two glaring flaws, one hypothetical and one very real. With foreign relations constantly in mind, the Japanese military and civilian authorities feared Britain or some other foreign power would intervene on behalf of China before Japan could seize Beijing.[xciii] The second, very real issue was that the sheer size of China, coupled with the weakness of the Qing Dynasty, meant that if Japan truly wanted victory, the war could go on indefinitely. Indeed, the Japanese would discover that was the case a generation later during its next war with China.[xciv]

In the shorter term, at least, the capture of Weihaiwei was the primary strategic objective, as it would cripple Chinese military operations and remove once and for all the threat of the Beiyang Fleet.[xcv] Both sides readied for a climactic battle, amassing troops and ships to defend or take the port. Chinese officials called for the port to surrender, but the defenders refused, and Japanese troops marched towards the Chinese Beiyang Fleet headquarters on January 26.[xcvi]

Slowed by Chinese assaults and lack of proper supply transport, the all-out assault did not begin until January 30.[xcvii] Japanese forces adopted a three-pronged assault on the south and east portions of the defenses. Despite the bitter cold and fierce winds, the Japanese pressed on, and, after roughly nine hours of battle, the Chinese abandoned the largely intact outward defenses.[xcviii] The Japanese suffered minor casualties, but they included Major General Ōdera Yasuzumi, the highest ranking casualty of the war for the Japanese. Nonetheless, the Japanese claimed the city on February 2.[xcix]

Major General Ōdera Yasuzumi

Utagawa Kokunimasa's print depicting the death of Major General Ōdera Yasuzumi
The Beiyang Fleet remained nearby, continually bombarding the Japanese as they holed up in

the harbor. It was not until the sea and winds calmed on February 3 that the Fleet's efforts came to light and a counter was possible. The Japanese responded, in a strategy repeated in their next war with a foreign power, by unleashing waves of torpedo boats against the Chinese fleet.[c] On February 12, the Chinese Admiral, Ding Ruchang, surrendered and committed suicide shortly after. His replacement ordered the scuttling of the remainder of the fleet and followed the example of his commanding officer by committing suicide.[ci]

The loss of Weihaiwei and of the Beiyang Fleet effectively ended China's ability to resist the Japanese navy. However, while the naval situation was handled, the Japanese army still faced the logistical nightmare of invading China, and with their forces spread from Manchuria to Port Arthur, the threat of a massive Chinese army overwhelming them loomed with each passing day.[cii]

While the Japanese consolidated their forces in Manchuria, the Chinese concentrated their forces to defend against the resumed Japanese offensive. A debate ensued between Japanese army commanders and the Imperial headquarters over whether the army should first attempt to wipe out the massing Chinese forces or move straight to Beijing.[ciii] The higher-ups believed such a mop-up operation would take too long and distract from the goal of Beijing, while the generals countered that as long as the Chinese had an army, they could fight even if Beijing fell. Eventually, a compromise was reached that called for the Japanese army to mop-up the Chinese in southern Manchuria, thus preventing a possible flanking maneuver as the army marched to Beijing.[civ]

For the first time in the war, the Chinese put the Japanese on the defensive, striking their forces in Manchuria to prevent their advance. Though brief, the Chinese efforts to halt the Japanese proved to be some of the toughest fighting in the war, in conjunction with the conditions brought on by a brutal winter.[cv]

The Battle of Yingkou, which occurred March 4, 1895, was part of the Chinese offensive to retake the city of Haicheng, the last of four such efforts by the Chinese in their only offensive campaign of the war.[cvi] Having lost Haicheng, the Chinese reinforced Yingkou with everything they could muster, and though it was a treaty port open to foreign powers, the Japanese nonetheless attacked it and, despite having to deal with stiff resistance by the Chinese, captured it by March 7.[cvii]

Depictions of the battle

Moving quickly, the Japanese engaged the Chinese again just two days later, assaulting a city across the Lao River to the northwest of Yingkou. Here the Chinese fought in the streets, and the Japanese, sensing victory was near, ruthlessly pressed forward, refusing to allow anyone to surrender and shooting at those attempting to flee the field.[cviii] As a final act of total war, the

Japanese razed the city of T'ienchuangt'ai to the ground with brutal efficiency. The Chinese retreated north, and the Japanese bunkered down for occupation duty.

The fighting in Manchuria was effectively over,[cix] but the war was not, and one theater in particular was proving to be a far greater headache than expected. The Japanese assault on Taiwan, intended as a sideshow to win the islands during the inevitable peace negotiations, proved far more difficult than intended. Known as the Pescadores Campaign for the islands near Taiwan, Japanese efforts to take the islands took place from March 23-25, 189.[cx] The Chinese offered little resistance, but, as so often happens in island campaigns, disease ravaged the soldiers. 25% of Japanese casualties came from such sicknesses, a testament to how understaffed and poorly supplied they were for the campaign.[cxi]

Thanks to the adventurer/reporter James W. Davidson, the brief Pescadores Campaign was carefully documented. While Japanese reporters focused on the mainland assaults, Davidson wrote extensively on the campaign:

"On March 20th, after a five days' trip from Sasebo naval station, the expedition, consisting of the fleet and the transports, arrived off the Pescadores and anchored near Pachau island to the south of the principal islands of the group. Bad weather on the 21st and 22nd prevented an immediate attack on the forts; but on the 23rd, the storm having abated, the ships got underway, and at 9.30 a.m., upon the first flying squadron drawing near Hau-chiau [候角?], the fleet subjected the Kon-peh-tai fort to a heavy bombardment, to which the Chinese replied for nearly an hour before they were silenced.

"During the afternoon, the disembarkation of the troops commenced. By the aid of steam pinnaces each towing several cutters, the troops, consisting of the 1st, 2nd, 3rd and 4th Companies of the 1st Regiment of reserves under the command of Colonel Hishijima, were all landed in less than two hours. The landing of the troops brought the Kon-peh-tai fort into action again, but without inflicting much damage on the Japanese. The troops on shore engaged in a skirmish with some 300 Chinese soldiers, afterward reinforced by 150 more, near a commanding knoll which both forces were desirous of occupying. After a few volleys from the Japanese, answered by an irregular fire from the Chinese, the latter eventually fled, leaving the position in the hands of the Japanese. Staff-quarters were then established in the village of Chien-shan [尖山社].

"At 2.30 on the morning of the 24th, the troops advanced with the intention of taking the Kon-peh-tai fort and Makung (Bako) with a temporary company of mountain artillery under Captain Arai and the naval contingent with quick firing guns under Naval Lieutenant Tajima in the van. The night was very dark and the only available route was so frequently cut up with ditches running in every direction that progress was laboriously slow; only some two miles being made after three hours of painful tramping. By about 4 a.m., the Japanese force had all reached the rallying ground, and thirty minutes later, led by the 2nd Battalion of the 1st Regiment of reserves, were advancing towards the fort. The 5th Company, under the command of Captain Kinoshita, formed the advance guard, and a detachment of this company, under command of Lieutenant Ishii, were the first to engage the Chinese forces, 200 of whom had taken up a position outside the fort and appeared to dispute the advance of the Japanese. The engagement was very brief, the Chinese flying before the small number of determined Japanese. Meanwhile, the temporary battery of mountain artillery had been shelling the fort from a position too far distant to do much damage to the stronghold, but in a manner sufficiently effective to frighten out the garrison, who left in such haste that, thirty minutes after the first gun had been fired, the Japanese were in possession. Thus was the principal port captured in the Pescadores.

"The naval contingent were also enabled to participate in the engagement, and with their two quick-firing guns did much execution. The 4th Company of the 1st Regiment of reserves and the naval contingent captured the village, after only a slight skirmish with the enemy. The place had been held by a garrison 500 strong. With the 2nd Company of the 1st Regiment of reserves leading the van, the Japanese forces now reassembled and advanced on the capital and principal city of the islands, Makung. No opposition was encountered on the way, with the exception of some ineffective firing from the Yui-wang island fort [漁翁島砲臺]; and upon reaching the city, the 1st Company stormed the Chinese infantry encampment, being followed soon after by the 2nd Company, which dashed through the gateway with the intention of dividing into three sections and attacking the enemy from different sides. But, to their amazement, their plans were found unnecessary, the garrison, with the exception of some thirty who did make a slight show of resistance, having fled. Some shots were fired at a few stragglers, and at 11.50 a.m. the occupation of the city was complete.

"Another engagement the same day resulted in the capture of the fort in the Yuan-ching peninsula [圓頂半島] by Commander Tanji with a naval force; about 500 of the enemy surrendering without making any resistance whatever. Two days later (March 26th), blue jackets occupied the Yui-wang island forts and found the place empty, the garrison having fled. Soon after the Japanese entered, a native presented himself, apparently on a very important mission, which proved to be the delivery of a letter stating that the Chinese commander and garrison wished to inform the Japanese that they surrendered the fort. Thus fell the key to Southern China.

"The Chinese prisoners, with the exception of eight officers, were given their liberty. The spoils of the little campaign were considerable, including 18 cannon, 2,663 rifles, over a million rounds of ammunition, 797 casks, and 3,173 bags of powder, a thousand bags of rice, etc., etc. Rear-Admiral Tanaka occupied the post of first governor of the group, and a government office and military post offices were at once erected."[cxii]

With the Pescadores Campaign concluded, the Chinese Navy destroyed, Manchuria occupied, and the Chinese army demoralized and hiding in the mountains, the Japanese were ready for the war to end. Loading up their military and civilian dignitaries, the Japanese prepared for a different kind of fight at the negotiating table.

Foreign Perspectives

Even before Japan and China went to war, Western powers looked warily upon Japan as the 19th century was ending, and upon the outbreak of war, Westerners became even more alarmed at Japan's rising ambitions in Asia, especially when those ambitions threatened those of the West.

France in particular passionately insisted on having the war end, as one scholar explained: "Around the time of the outbreak of the First Sino-Japanese War, France reiterated that it had no direct interest in the Korean issue, and professed to be an onlooker. But from the very beginning, in fact, France viewed the war as an opportunity to consolidate its alliance with Russia and further encroach on China's southwest frontiers; it was therefore happy to see war break out between China and Japan, and took Russia's position on stopping Britain from playing a dominant role in mediation between them. As the outcome of the war became clear, exposing Japan's ambition to invade China, France turned from its wait-and-see attitude to intervention, taking an active part in the peacemaking activities of Russia, Britain and France and the triple intervention of Russia, France and Germany. In so doing, it attempted to safeguard general European interests and consolidate its alliance with Russia, as well as preventing Japan from replacing Europe as the dominant force in China. At the same time, it demanded a quid pro quo from the victim. During negotiation over the return of the Liaodong Peninsula, France put aside its conflicts with its old enemy Germany and endeavored to mediate in disputes between Germany and Russia so as to maintain concerted action under the triple intervention. It proposed to sacrifice the interests of China to satisfy the wishes of Japan and Russia for a swift resolution of the issue of the Liaodong Peninsula."[cxiii]

Besides improving relations with Russia, France also kept in mind its own holdings in Indochina. A weakened China meant a stronger hold on the region for France, which had gone to war with China the previous decade. In particular, France hoped to define the border of Vietnam in the most advantageous way possible, and a weak China presented the best opportunity to do so.[cxiv] At the same time, a stronger Japan threatened Indochina, necessitating a careful balance for France of a weak China, a pacified Japan, and a friendly Russia.

The aims of the United States were more long-term. Though concern over the fate of Hawaii loomed in many American minds, the fate of America in the Pacific in the future also weighed heavily. As one American official put it, "There is no occasion for fuss or bluster, but there is a need for an inflexible backbone. The foreign policy of the United States is simplicity in itself. We draw a line around the globe taking in the middle of the Pacific on the west and the middle of the Atlantic on the east. Within that line our interests and our influence are paramount... European and Asian powers can avoid all chance of collision with us by simply following our example."[cxv]

The Port Arthur Massacre in particular generated interest in the West, even as the Japanese generally ignored Western concerns. Regarding the massacre, an article in the *Los Angeles Times* summed up the American position: "It cannot be said that the fall of Port Arthur was unexpected at the State Department, although the officials had supposed that it would have withstood a protracted siege... It is the opinion of military experts that Japan's attack on Port Arthur was a most perilous effort on their part. They could not afford to sustain any considerable defeat for the result would have been, in the first place, to determine the Chinese to pursue the war, and in the second place, to retard the Japanese government in its efforts to float a new war loan. But by the victory at Port Arthur the success of the latter is now assured."[cxvi]

The American press also reported on the sinking of the British vessel loaded with Chinese soldiers: "In five minutes the stern began to sink but it was half an hour before the *Kowshing* plunged out of sight in the midst of what looked like a crowded swimming pool at a Chinese lunatic asylum. When the *Naniwa* opened fire, some of the Chinese troops popped back harmlessly with their hand pieces... Like dozens of the *Titanic's,* passengers, many of the Chinese, especially those unable to swim, still were unconvinced that the solid-feeling vessel could be less secure than the deep ocean, and they remained on board until the last... the half-crazed soldiers on the topside of [the] doomed ship were shooting at [Captain] Galsworthy and even at their comrades in the water and well as at the enemy. Togo could not prudently lower any rescue boats until the futile firing from the *Kowshing* had ceased and she was about to go under...Then he despatched [sic] two cutters. They picked up only Galsworthy and two others, neither Chinese. This selectivity was difficult to ascribe and it circumstantially corroborated the atrocity stories of the deliberate massacre by rifle and machine-gun fire upon the men struggling in the water. A couple of the *Kowshing's* lifeboats deliberately were sunk. Those shipless Chinamen not slain by the bullets were left to flounder in the water. Most of them followed their transport to Davy Jones's locker... The credible evidence compels the ugly conclusion not only that the boat-crews violated every canon of seafaring chivalry but also that the cold-blooded slaughter was committed by some of the gun crews aboard the cruiser."[cxvii]

Though the United States did not intervene during the war as Great Britain did, nor did America intervene at its end as France and Russia did, the AMericans did keep a close eye on the war and Japan's actions throughout. As one scholar noted regarding the American view of the war, officials vacillated "from believing the Japanese to be set for defeat due to the size and overwhelming manpower of China, to the possibility of a Japanese victory given their remarkable fighting ability, to the condemnation of Japanese atrocities from out of control soldiers, to the lauding of Japan's superiority and Western-like mindset, to an empathy with the Japanese over their losses at the force of European intervention, to a fear of Japanese military might and vengeance."[cxviii] The United States would keep a careful eye on Japan's progress as it continued to expand, and the ramifications would become obvious during World War II.

Great Britain's interests in the region were mostly tied to China, and from those interests blossomed the broader international scope of the war and its consequences, as Japan sought to defend itself against accusations of violating international law.[cxix] In the end, as one historian noted, "Japan's strategic use of force in the Sino-Japanese War of 1894-95 eventually confirmed the legitimacy and authority of Japan as a sovereign power. Within five years of the war - by 1899 - Japanese conduct during the war had become the subject of an international legal presentation, which was intended: (1) to confirm that Japan waged war in a manner conforming to international law; (2) to affirm that Japan had attained the civilization and moral ideals common among the family of nations; and (3) to reaffirm Britain's confidence in having renegotiated a treaty with Japan that was befitting of Japan's equal and sovereign status. In short, the intersection of the Sino-Japanese War and international law underlined Japan's success at having reconstructed itself as a sovereign state."[cxx]

Though it was important to how Japan presented itself internationally, in the end the semantics of international law mattered little when Japan was finally ready to negotiate terms with China. Having inflicted defeat after defeat on the once mighty Qing Dynasty, Japan expected to dominate the negotiations with China, at least until the West intervened, as many Japanese officials predicted.

Peace Negotiations

As early as November of 1894, the Chinese tried to enter peace negotiations with the Japanese, but the Japanese refused until the spring of 1895, intent on maximizing their gains.[cxxi] Pressured by Western powers, which, with the exception of the British, had largely stayed out of the war, the Japanese entered a cease-fire on March 27.[cxxii]

Foreshadowing the kind of difficulties that would plague the Japanese military for decades, the negotiators were their own worst enemies. The navy and army both had differing opinions on what Japan should demand from China - the Army wanted the Liaotung peninsula to better defend Korea against Chinese assault, considering Korea's status as a Japanese protectorate to now be a given,[cxxiii] but the navy wanted Taiwan, reflecting a desire to expand its power, just as the army's goals would extend theirs.

Civilian officials were also divided. Believing Russia would intervene if Japan took Manchuria, some officials suggested an indemnity from China instead of territory, but others argued that because of Russian aggression Japan should take Manchuria and an indemnity.[cxxiv] Those in the financial know desired a massive indemnity China would never be able to afford. Still others wanted everything, from Manchuria and Taiwan to a hefty indemnity, and even the entire Chinese coast.[cxxv] Those who warned of angering the Chinese and destroying the ability to garner good relations in the future with such harsh demands went unheeded.

The West, in response to Japanese ambitions, mobilized to intervene on China's behalf. Russia in particular made it very clear that while they had no issue with Japan claiming Taiwan, they would take issue should Japan claim Manchuria.[cxxvi] Despite such warnings, Japan continued to press for territory in Manchuria, and various officials in Japan, among them Yamagata, believed relations with Russia good enough that the Tsar would not press the issue further than stern words.[cxxvii]

Thus, the Japanese opened negotiations by demanding the Liaotung peninsula, Taiwan and the Pescadores Islands, an indemnity to cover Japan's war expenses, Chinese recognition of Korean independence, and a commitment to negotiate an unequal commercial treaty in the Western style.[cxxviii] The Chinese negotiator struggled to temper Japanese ambitions, stating that the two nations should stand united against Western influence and not pick at each other for the bits left over by the world's strongest powers. China, however, had no real room to negotiate unless a Western power intervened directly, and so far, none had. The Japanese, conceding little, reduced their land desires to the Yalu River in Manchuria, and they reduced the indemnity from 300 to 200 Chinese taels, or 200 million yen. With no room to negotiate, and the Japanese army eager and willing to march on Beijing if needed, the Chinese agreed to the new terms, signing the peace treaty on April 17, 1895.[cxxix] The Treaty of Shimonoseki read:

"Article 1: China recognizes definitively the full and complete independence and autonomy of Korea, and, in consequence, the payment of tribute and the performance of ceremonies and formalities by Korea to China, that are in derogation of such independence and autonomy, shall wholly cease for the future.

"Articles 2 & 3: China cedes to Japan in perpetuity and full sovereignty of the Pescadores group, Formosa (Taiwan) and the eastern portion of the bay of Liaodong Peninsula together with all fortifications, arsenals and public property.

"Article 4: China agrees to pay to Japan as a war indemnity the sum of 200,000,000 Kuping taels (7,500,000 kilograms/16,534,500 pounds of silver).

"Article 5: China opens Shashih, Chungking, Soochow and Hangchow to Japan. Moreover, China is to grant Japan most favored nation status for foreign trade."[cxxx]

The ink had barely dried on the treaty when the West finally intervened. Diplomats from Russia, France, and Germany arrived on April 23 to urge Japan to reconsider their acquisitions in Manchuria. Japan attempted to appeal to Great Britain and the United States, but both nations, opposing the war from the start and unwilling to go against the Tsar, the Third Republic, and the Kaiser, forced Japan to concede its land claims in Manchuria for an extra 30 million taels. With the threat of Western influence, international isolation, and financial crises, the war finally ended.[cxxxi]

As the First Sino-Japanese War finished, Russia was breathing down both the backs of both nations, France was increasingly wary of threats to Indochina, Germany was gradually entering international politics, and Britain and America remained somewhat alarmed by the new empire's rise. Having faced little real opposition, the Japanese emerged in high spirits. It would take more objective observers to consider the full scope of the war's effects, and even decades for its full repercussions to reach fruition.

The Aftermath of War
Every war, even a victorious one, needs its fallen heroes to glorify the cause for the people. The extolling of the common soldier and sailor exemplifies the cost of war from the bottom up, and Japan was no exception to this.

For the navy, there came a song, titled simply "The Valiant Sailor":
> No trace of smoke or cloud, nor breath of wind or wave
> Yet what is it that begins to cloud the mirrorlike surface of the Yellow Sea?
> What is this strange thunder in the air? This lightning flashing over the waves?
> Smoke rises into the sky, darkening the face of the sun
> In the heat of the battle the decks are dyed scarlet
> With the noble blood of those brave men who gave their all
> Amid bursting shot and shell a sailor lies, body riddled with wounds
> Holding on to life's thread with but the fierceness of his courage
> His wounded gaze fixes upon the First Officer passing by
> And raising an agonized voice he shouts, "Commander!"
> So summoned, the First Officer pauses by his side
> And the sailor gasps out, "Isn't the *Dingyuan* sunk yet?"
> The First Officer's eyes glisten with tears, but with manly voice he replies,
> "Rest easy. The *Dingyuan* won't put up much more of a fight."
> Hearing this, a last, happy smile passes over the sailor's lips
> "Go get 'em for me," he says, and draws his final breath.
> No enemy can stand against the faithful forces of our imperial land
> The noble banner of the Rising Sun unfurls, illuminating the Eastern Seas
> "Isn't the *Dingyuan* sunk yet?" These words, though brief
> Shall long be written in the hearts of all who love our noble land[cxxxii]

For the Army, their hero was a bugler whose sacrifice for the empire was also retold in song. Titled "The Bugle's Echo," the version presented below, though somewhat liberally translated, reflects the spirit of the lyrics better than the more literal translation presented of the previous song:
> Easy in other time than this
> Were Anjo's stream to cross;
> But now, beneath the storm of shot,
> Its waters seethe and toss.
>
> In other time to pass that stream
> Were sport for boys at play;
> But every man through blood must wade
> Who fords Anjo to-day.
>
> The bugle sounds; -through flood and flame
> Charges the line of steel; -
> Above the crash of battle rings
> The bugle's stern appeal.

Why has the bugle ceased to call?
Why does it call once more?
Why sounds the stirring signal now
More faintly than before?

What time the bugle ceased to sound, the breast was smitten through; -
What time the blast rang faintly, blood
Gushed from the lips that blew.
Death-stricken, still the bugler stands!
He leans upon his gun, -
Once more to sound the bugle-call
Before his life be done.

What though the shattered body fail?
The spirit rushes free
Through Heaven and Earth to sound anew
Tat call to Victory!

Far, far beyond our shores the spot
No honored by his fall; -
But forty million brethren
Have heard that bugle-call.
Comrade! –Beyond the peaks and seas
Your bugle sounds to-day
In forty million loyal hearts
A thousand miles away![cxxxiii]

    Though honoring the sacrifices of the dead is important for any nation, especially one that honors its ancestors like the Japanese, in the end the war's victors reap the full glory of the war and its resultant laurels. Emperor Meiji, the nominal commander of the military, was hailed as a hero for his success in commanding the Japanese military. A triumphal arch was built for a spectacular parade in which he and a retinue of police, cavalry, and other officials marched.[cxxxiv] Furthermore, the war solidified the emperor's place in modern Japanese politics. Viewed as ruling by divine right, the emperor loomed above the petty politicking of those below, which also served to isolate him from the government in general.[cxxxv] The war also reflected poorly on the Diet, whose taxes burdened the blue collar workers and increased the divide between rich and poor, a problem the Diet would fail to shake even into the modern era.[cxxxvi]

    Though nationally the war did succeed in uniting the people, however briefly, it clearly failed to do so outside of Japan's borders. Japan's efforts destroyed relations with the Koreans, compelling Korea to look to Russia as a new counterweight.[cxxxvii] China also turned to Russia, and increasingly France, to pay off the indemnity. In exchange for the loans, Russia gained railway access through Manchuria to Vladivostok, paving the way for war with the Japanese in the coming decade.[cxxxviii] Moreover, China started hiring German military advisors to bolster their clearly inadequate military training.

    Though Japan now stood as a legitimate power in foreign eyes, it was also viewed with suspicion and fear.[cxxxix] At the same time, the Japanese were ambivalent about Western viewpoints. Notions of bushido and imperial might germinated in Japan, and the military began hefty expansion programs with the aims of developing enough military might to dictate terms in Asia and possess enough naval power to fend off a European alliance.[cxl] As both the army and navy expanded, the two services' rivalry continued. The civilian government increasingly sided with the navy, to the detriment of everyone.[cxli]

Culturally, the war brought about a new period of militant nationalism in Japan, and its economy became increasingly geared toward military expansion and development. Bolstered by the Chinese indemnity, the economy surged, infrastructure spread out across the islands, and, as with any industrial growth, crime and yellow journalism expanded as well.[cxlii] The focus on the military assured that Japanese children's education became increasingly militarized, affecting their learning structure, what they learned, and even their uniforms (the sailor uniforms so fancied by Western fans of Japanese culture are a lingering reminder of this new era in Japanese expansion).[cxliii]

Flush with war money, victory, and a new century looming on the horizon, Japan entered a new era in its history, but about half a century later, this focus on militaristic nationalism would slowly consume it to a point that nearly destroyed the nation. Japan's expansion in the 1930s would lead to atrocities that would've been unthinkable even to those who witnessed the First Sino-Japanese War or the Russo-Japanese War, and of course, the ensuing horrors of World War II, ending with the use of atomic weapons on Hiroshima and Nagasaki, can also be traced back to the victories over China in the First Sino-Japanese War.

Online Resources

Other Asian history titles by Charles River Editors

Other titles about the Sino-Japanese Wars on Amazon

Further Reading

Chang, Jung (2013). The Concubine Who Launched Modern China: Empress Dowager Cixi. New York: Anchor Books. ISBN 9780307456700.

Duus, Peter (1998). The Abacus and the Sword: The Japanese Penetration of Korea. University of California Press. ISBN 0-520-92090-2.

Schencking, J. Charles (2005). Making Waves: Politics, Propaganda, And The Emergence Of The Imperial Japanese Navy, 1868–1922. Stanford University Press. ISBN 0-8047-4977-9.

Keene, Donald (2002). Emperor of Japan: Meiji and His World, 1852–1912. New York: Columbia University Press. ISBN 0-231-12341-8.

Evans, David C; Peattie, Mark R (1997). Kaigun: strategy, tactics, and technology in the Imperial Japanese Navy, 1887–1941. Annapolis, Maryland: Naval Institute Press. ISBN 0-87021-192-7.

Jansen, Marius B. (2002). The Making of Modern Japan. Harvard University Press. ISBN 0-674-00334-9.

Jansen, Marius B. (1995). The Emergence of Meiji Japan. Cambridge University Press. ISBN 0-521-48405-7.

Jowett, Philip (2013). China's Wars: Rousing the Dragon 1894-1949. Bloomsbury Publishing. ISBN 1-47280-673-5.

Kim, Chong Ik Eugene, and Han-kyo Kim. ;;Korea and the Politics of Imperialism, 1876-1910 (Univ of California Press, 1967).

Kwang-Ching, Liu (1978). John King Fairbank, ed. The Cambridge History of China. Volume 11, Late Ch'ing, 1800–1911 Part 2 (illustrated ed.). Cambridge University Press. ISBN 0-521-22029-7.

Lone, Stewart (1994). Japan's First Modern War: Army and Society in the Conflict with China,

1894–1895. New York: St. Martin's Press.

Mutsu, Munemitsu. (1982). Kenkenroku (trans. Gordon Mark Berger). Tokyo: University of Tokyo Press. ISBN 978-0-86008-306-1; OCLC 252084846

Morse, Hosea Ballou. (1918). The international relations of the Chinese empire vol 2 1861–1893

Morse, Hosea Ballou. (1918). The international relations of the Chinese empire vol 3 1894–1916

Olender, Piotr (2014). Sino-Japanese Naval War 1894–1895. MMPBooks. ISBN 83-63678-30-9.

Paine, S.C.M (2003). The Sino-Japanese War of 1894–1895: Perceptions, Power, and Primacy. Cambridge University Press. ISBN 0-521-81714-5.

Palais, James B. (1975). Politics and Policy in Traditional Korea. Harvard University Asia Center. ISBN 0-674-68770-1.

Sondhaus, Lawrence (2001). Naval Warfare, 1815–1914. Routledge. ISBN 0-415-21477-7.

Zachmann, Urs Matthias (2009). China and Japan in the Late Meiji Period: China Policy and the Japanese Discourse on National Identity, 1895-1904. Routledge. ISBN 0415481910.

Free Books by Charles River Editors

We have brand new titles available for free most days of the week. To see which of our titles are currently free, click on this link.

Discounted Books by Charles River Editors

We have titles at a discount price of just 99 cents everyday. To see which of our titles are currently 99 cents, click on this link.

---

[i] Lone, Stewart, *Japan's First Modern War: Army and Society in the Conflict with China, 1894–1895*, New York: St. Martin's Press (1994), pg. 15.
[ii] Ibid, 14.
[iii] Ibid, 15.
[iv] Ibid, 15.
[v] Ibid, 15.
[vi] Ibid, 15.
[vii] Makito, Saya, trans. Noble, D., *The Sino-Japanese War and the Birth of Japanese Nationalism*, I-House Press, Tokyo, (2011), pg. 13.
[viii] The Emperor essentially serving as a puppet with no real power, though still an extremely esteemed and venerated figure.
[ix] Ibid, 14.
[x] Lone, Stewart, *Japan's First Modern War*, pg. 15.
[xi] Ibid, 15.
[xii] Ibid, 15.
[xiii] Ibid, 15-16.
[xiv] Ibid, 15-16.
[xv] China's External Relations –A History, Convention of Tientsin (Tianjin), 1885, accessed January 28, 2018, http://www.chinaforeignrelations.net/node/176
[xvi] Lone, Stewart, *Japan's First Modern War*, pg. 16-17.
[xvii] Ibid, 16-17.
[xviii] Ibid, 17.
[xix] Ibid, 17.
[xx] Ibid, 17-18.
[xxi] Ibid, 18.
[xxii] Ibid, 18.

[xxiii] Ni Tao, "Defeat in first Sino-Japanese war a turning point that shocked China", Aug 5, 2014, accessed January 29, 2018, https://www.shine.cn/archive/feature/art-and-culture/Defeat-in-first-SinoJapanese-war-a-turning-point-that-shocked-China/shdaily.shtml
[xxiv] Ibid.
[xxv] Lone, Stewart, *Japan's First Modern War*, pg. 19.
[xxvi] Ibid, 20.
[xxvii] Ibid, 20.
[xxviii] Ibid, 20-21.
[xxix] Ibid, 21.
[xxx] Ibid, 21.
[xxxi] Quoted in Ibid, 24.
[xxxii] Ibid, 24.
[xxxiii] Ibid, 24.
[xxxiv] Ibid, 24.
[xxxv] Ibid, 24-25.
[xxxvi] Ibid, 25.
[xxxvii] Ibid, 25.
[xxxviii] Ibid, 25-26.
[xxxix] Quoted in Ibid, 26.
[xl] Ibid, 25-26, Makito, Saya, trans. Noble, D., *The Sino-Japanese War*, pg. 18.
[xli] Lone, Stewart, *Japan's First Modern War*, pg. 26.
[xlii] Ibid, 27.
[xliii] Ibid, 27.
[xliv] Ibid, 28.
[xlv] Quoted in Ibid, 28.
[xlvi] Ibid, 28-29.
[xlvii] Quoted in Ibid, 29.
[xlviii] Ibid, 27.
[xlix] Ibid, 27-29.
[l] Hastings, Max, *The Korean War*, Pan Books (2007), pg. 24-25.
[li] Lone, Stewart, *Japan's First Modern War*, pg. 30.
[lii] Ibid, 31.
[liii] Ibid, 33.
[liv] Ibid, 33.
[lv] Ibid, 33.
[lvi] Ibid, 33.
[lvii] Ibid, 34.
[lviii] Makito, Saya, trans. Noble, D., *The Sino-Japanese War*, pg. 26.
[lix] Ibid, 26.
[lx] Quoted in Ibid, 27-28.
[lxi] Ibid, 28.
[lxii] Ibid, 33.
[lxiii] Ibid, 33.
[lxiv] Ibid, 33-34.
[lxv] Lone, Stewart, *Japan's First Modern War*, pg. 34.
[lxvi] Paine, S.C.M, *The Sino-Japanese War of 1894–1895: Perception, Power, and Primacy*, Cambridge University Press (2003), pg. 158.
[lxvii] Lone, Stewart, *Japan's First Modern War*, pg. 34-35.
[lxviii] Ibid, 35.
[lxix] Ibid, 35.
[lxx] Ibid, 35.
[lxxi] Ibid, 35.
[lxxii] Ibid, 36.
[lxxiii] Ibid, 36.
[lxxiv] Ibid, 36-37.

[lxxv] Ibid, 37.
[lxxvi] Ni Tao, "Defeat in first Sino-Japanese war a turning point that shocked China", accessed February 6, 2018.
[lxxvii] Ibid.
[lxxviii] Ibid.
[lxxix] Lone, Stewart, *Japan's First Modern War*, pg. 38.
[lxxx] Ibid, 38.
[lxxxi] Ibid, 38. Not to be confused with the naval battle that occurred at the Yalu earlier in the year and was not mentioned previously due to the broader strokes of this article.
[lxxxii] Ibid, 38-39.
[lxxxiii] Ibid, 39.
[lxxxiv] Ibid, 39.
[lxxxv] Ibid, 39.
[lxxxvi] Ibid, 39.
[lxxxvii] Makito, Saya, trans. Noble, D., *The Sino-Japanese War*, pg. 44.
[lxxxviii] Ibid, 44.
[lxxxix] Ibid, 44.
[xc] Ibid, 45-46.
[xci] Ibid, 46.
[xcii] Lone, Stewart, *Japan's First Modern War*, pg. 44.
[xciii] Ibid, 164-165.
[xciv] Ibid, 165.
[xcv] Ibid, 166.
[xcvi] Ibid, 166.
[xcvii] Ibid, 166.
[xcviii] Ibid, 166.
[xcix] Ibid, 166.
[c] Ibid, 166-167.
[ci] Ibid, 167.
[cii] Ibid, 167.
[ciii] Ibid, 168.
[civ] Ibid, 168.
[cv] Ibid, 169.
[cvi] Ibid, 169.
[cvii] Ibid, 169.
[cviii] Ibid, 169.
[cix] Ibid, 169.
[cx] Paine, S.C.M, *The Sino-Japanese War of 1894-1895*, pg. 264. Not to be confused with the Pescadores Campaign of the French-Sino War that occurred in the decade preceding this war.
[cxi] Lone, Stewart, *Japan's First Modern War*, pg. 170.
[cxii] Davidson, James W., *The Island of Formosa, Past and Present*, London and New York: Macmillan (1903), pg. 266-268.
[cxiii] Ge Fuping (2015) "France and the First Sino-Japanese War, 1894-1895," Social Sciences in China, 36:4, 138-139.
[cxiv] Ibid, 143.
[cxv] Hough, Kenneth C., "Brazen throat of war: The California press reaction to the Sino-Japanese War and the growth of Japanese militarism, 1894–1895", 2004, pg. 146.
[cxvi] Ibid, 99.
[cxvii] Ibid, 91.
[cxviii] Ibid, 146.
[cix] Howland, Douglas, "Japan's Civilized War: International Law as Diplomacy in the Sino-Japanese War (1894–1895)", Journal of the History of International Law / Revue d'histoire du droit international, 2007, Volume 9, Issue 2, pg. 179.
[cxx] Ibid, 186-187.
[cxxi] Lone, Stewart, *Japan's First Modern War*, pg. 171.
[cxxii] Ibid, 172.

[cxxiii] Ibid, 172.
[cxxiv] Ibid, 172.
[cxxv] Ibid, 172.
[cxxvi] Ibid, 173-174.
[cxxvii] Ibid, 174.
[cxxviii] Ibid, 174. Presumably a kitchen sink was also considered but dropped due to the lack of Chinese industry at the time.
[cxxix] Ibid, 175.
[cxxx] The Treaty of Shimonoseki, http://www.taiwanbasic.com/treaties/Shimonoseki.htm, accessed February 12, 2018.
[cxxxi] Ibid, 176.
[cxxxii] Makito, Saya, trans. Noble, D., *The Sino-Japanese War*, pg. 53-54.
[cxxxiii] Quoted in Ibid, 59-60.
[cxxxiv] Quoted in Ibid, 114-115.
[cxxxv] Lone, Stewart, *Japan's First Modern War*, pg. 178.
[cxxxvi] Ibid, 179.
[cxxxvii] Ibid, 179.
[cxxxviii] Ibid, 179.
[cxxxix] Ibid, 179-180.
[cxl] Ibid, 182.
[cxli] Ibid, 182.
[cxlii] Ibid, 184-185.
[cxliii] Ibid, 186